Separation SEO: 101 Ways to Trump Your Competition and Triple Your Web Traffic

Table of Contents

What is SEO?

SEO is an acronym of "Search Engine Optimization". It is a process of making sure that the natural ability of website is affected positively when it comes to organic or unpaid search of the engines like Google, Bing, Yahoo and other engines that are working in this regard. It is directly related t keywords and makes sure that it appears in the search results more than one time so that more visitors as well as revenue is generate for the website. However this is not the only target of the SEO as the other features include video and image searches that are boosted to increase the traffic and to make sure that the best is provided to the site owners as well as visitors in terms of site appearance as well as its rankings.

Web presence is something that is also a part of SEO however the SEO as a whole is never considered to be a part of web presence as it is a different and complete phenomenon within itself. Web presence on the other hand makes sure that how active a site is when it comes to different activities it is indulged in. the overall idea of web presence is multi-dimensional as it includes social media, blogging and other activities that are considered to be life line of any website and related organization. The web presence also includes different marketing tactics that are carried out to make sure that the site is boosted and helps SEO to increase its effectiveness.

SEO is a smart science which never works on itself as it is always supported by the intelligence and the overall work that is carried out by the SEO specialist as well as analyst. It includes editing the HTML content of the website specifically the META tag and to minimize or totally remove the indexing activities of the search engines. It also targets the users through the use of keywords that the search engines like their users to enter to make sure that the best results are fetched. SEO specialist or optimizer is considered to be a guru if he is able to rank the website on the first page of search engines and if we talk of today then specifically Google. The latest research results show that almost 90% of traffic from all over the world is directed through the Google which makes it the largest search engine of the world. SEO categories are therefore divided on the basis of Google's behavior and they are termed as black hat SEO technique and white hat SEO techniques. Black hat SEO techniques are those which are not approved by any search engine and in some cases they are also considered to be as a crime for instance using the text similar to background color of the website or placing it off screen. In both cases it is considered to be as a crime by the search engines and they make sure that either the ranking are reduced or they are eliminated from the database altogether. Here the best example is that of BMW Germany that was removed from Google's rankings for using the black hat SEO techniques and resultantly they were banned by the internet giant however the management of BMW quickly apologized removed the pages and was restored once again. This also shows that strictness of the policies of the Google irrespective of company size and popularity so black hat techniques are never advised. Google should be the centre point of all SEO specialists and the businesses that are trying to implement the strategies related to organic search results.

Ways of improving the SEO and web presence of a business or website

There are tens of thousands of ways of making sure that the best is provided to the website as well as the associated business when it comes to search engine results. This e-book will make sure that the ways of improving the search results are mentioned in the very best form so that users can use all or some of the methods to determine the fate of the website for its good. Let's start with the methods that are so common that businesses have altogether eliminated their use. These methods are also to be considered as a check list before launching any ecommerce website. It will boost the rankings and will also make sure that the search results are never affected in this regard. The practicing of not applying these tactics is due to the fact that these tactics are very challenging and the results are also not shown instantly but an SEO optimizer or specialist should remember that these tasks are fruitful in the long run and the effects of these ideas also remain there for the website over a longer period of time making sure that the services are boosted in the search engine rankings as well as more users are attracted within a shorter period of time. Good SEO does not only include the best search results for the website but it also focuses on the ways in which a business can enhance the user experience. Every business should keep one point in consideration while applying different SEO tactics and that is to make it clear that that internet user are smart and they are becoming smart with every passing day so it is important for the SEO specialist to put forward the techniques that enhance the user experience while they are on the website. Failing to comply with this basic need of the user will result is something that is fatal and even the first page rankings are of no use if there is a general perception among the internet community that a specific business website is not attractive or it is very hard to get to the required section. Making and SEO friendly website should not be the only task of the business but it should also be user friendly so that the best results are attained from customer service perspective and website ranking is boosted. Once this technique is applied successfully users are automatically attracted towards the website and in the long run there is no need of any SEO at all. But in order to reach that point it is very important to make sure that the strategic approach is adopted so that the SEO charges can be reduced to minimum and the factor of cost effectiveness can be attained.

1. Link structuring

A website has more than one URL and at every location there exists a product or service of the company so in order to make sure that the best is derived in terms of traffic a website owner or developer should make sure that the URL's are such that they drive traffic to the website and this can be done with the help of keywords inclusion within each page that belong to the category on that page or the product that has been mentioned in this regard. Best link building strategy is one that connects the home page with hot selling items page directly.

2. On page optimization

Google keyword is perhaps the best tool that can be used to make sure that the best results are obtained in terms of keyword research. It is also to make sure that the industry specific keywords are not only pointed out but they are also applied to the website to drive traffic. Making page titles effective and targeted also serve the purpose in this regard and makes sure that the more people visit a particular page while they search for a specific keyword. One of the best ways to increase the effectiveness of the phenomenon it is advised to update the content regularly.

3. Image search

SEO specialist should not only focus on text but the images should also be added as a part of SEO strategy to make sure that the text that is included within the images is also optimized to increase the rankings as well as to make sure that the best is achieved in terms of SEO and targeted search of the user. Image search includes filenames and surrounding text both which makes sure that increase in traffic is done without any issue and according to human psychology images are more attractive and compelling as compared to text and other data forms.

4. Analyzing the keywords

It makes sure that the best is obtained in terms of keyword search and the targets that have been defined by the business. However it is an ongoing process and does not stop because there keyword shifting is very obvious on daily basis and for the same reason keyword analyzers should be used to serve the purpose. There are tens of thousands of keyword analyzers that are updated every day making sure that that the website owners can determine the shift in a very precise manner. It is therefore advised to use more than one keyword analyzer to get the best results resulting in website optimization.

5. Thin content is not permitted

In simple language thin content is something that has little or no value to the product or the website that is being promoted. Google has made the rules stricter and for the same reason manual action page is added to the website if thin content is detected. SEO specialist should detect the duplicate content, doorway pages as well as scraped content to make sure that the optimization is done in the best way making Google as well as the site owners happy and contented in terms of good and state of the art SEO.

6. Keyword research

There is a difference between keyword search and research so the SEO specialist should make sure that they are never mixed in any case. Keyword research leads a business to choose the best and targeted options and keywords for the website and this research is never conducted in a day or two. Continuous working is needed in this regard to make sure that the best and most refined results are applied in the best manner. It will not only give the best SEO view but will also make sure that the way people searching for any product are revealed so that the pages are optimized accordingly.

7. Quality matters

From website development to SEO quality is something that is always centralized in this regard. It makes sure that the website owners are not only happy with their website but the search engines also welcome them on their first pages. Content development, white hat SEO and targeted keyword optimization are some of the tools that make sure to get the best in this regard. If quality is maintained throughout then getting traffic for the website is never a big deal. Just analyze the large websites of the world like Facebook and Wikipedia and you will find that the only thing which they provide is quality in terms of services and products they offer to their customers.

8. Boosting user experience

It has been mentioned earlier that 90% of the internet traffic of the world comes from Google and it has just changed the rules for website rankings and on page optimizations. Now Google and the other search engines never rank the website based on the keywords and search results. Instead they also consider the user experience and the overall benefit that they get from a particular website. Website administrators can also play their part in this regard and can make sure that top notch services are provided to all the users so that they can leave good comments on the blog which in turn are used by the search engines to rank the websites.

9. Using Google Webmaster

A business can track the changes in the industry by making sure that they are being viewed all the time. This would also help them to track the changes in the best possible manner on real time basis. Google Webmaster is the largest and most effective tool that is present in this regard. It is therefore advised to all SEO specialists to get the best out of this tool by making sure that it is being used in the most effective manner. This tool also makes sure that each and every inch of the website is analyzed fully and thus it reveals the results that are in the best interest of the website's SEO.

10. Quality back links

It is one of the best tactics that boost the website rankings when it comes to SEO. Adding links from highly repute resources make sure that the search engines analyze this factor before the results are produced for any keyword. Highly reputed back links will make sure that the website is ranked at the best number and it will also allow the search engines to decide about the other factors that are related to user experience as well as anchor text. SEO campaign should include back links as the first and foremost priority so that the rankings are boosted in the best possible way.

11. Making website user friendly

Instead of making website SEO friendly it is very important for the developers to make a website that is user friendly. All the factors that govern the overall strategy of the SEO are interrelated and one cannot be considered as complete without other. A user friendly website will bring good reviews from the users as they would be able to search for the related pages and the products in a quite good manner leading to awesome results and will also act as a decisive factor in this regard that would make the search engines believe that the user experience related to ay website is at its peak.

12. Physical location of the server

It is one of the most important but less known factors in relation to SEO. Google and other search engines target the physical location of the servers and it is also used as one of the factor to rank the website. It is therefore advised to host the website in that country which is preferred by the search engines for instance USA, Canada, Australia and EU. At times the physical location of the server is not given any importance and the website is ranked in the company's own country keeping in view the factor of cost effectiveness. A business should always consider the fact that more spending means awesome results and vice versa. If this factor is considered then a positive SEO impacts awaits.

13. Update the content regularly

Google and the search engines make sure that the best is provided to the users all the time when they search for any related stuff or keyword. In addition to all this it is very important to note that the rankings are not only based on relevancy. The Google and other web giants present the pages that are user friendly and are created fresh. It is therefore the part of the SEO strategy to make sure that the unique and awesome content is produced all the time and the process never stops. Freshness of the content is something that is always considered by the search engines while displaying the pages.

14. Website Speed

The latest Panda Update that has been added by the Google to its algorithms has made the competition tougher. Hence the factor of website speed at which it loads different pages has also been made a part of the plan. It is therefore very important for the SEO specialist to keep the landing and home pages at the best in terms of speed and usability because the search engines will test the usability while displaying the pages as a result. The Panda Update has therefore compelled the website owners to get speedy pages on top and to optimize the website for the best user viewing.

15. Social media activities

It was suspected in the past that the search engines are using the social media data to rank the pages but it was denied. Finally few months back the Google has admitted that it is using the social media data to rank the pages and therefore it is very important for the website owners to get good rankings on the social media. Facebook and Google+ are recommended in this regard as they make sure that the pages directly appear in the search results and therefore good social media fan following is something that is very important in this regard.

16. Call to actions

The landing page of the website should have a clear call to action to make sure that the results are provided in the best possible manner. In simple words the call to actions should be used in a precise definite manner and should also be placed strategically over all the pages so that the users can see them and act upon if they wish. It has also been estimated that if the turn out in terms of call to action is 3% to 4% then the rankings are affected very positively and they are also used in the best possible way by the search engines to rank the website.

17. Sensibly rank the bestselling items

Each and every website that has been created focuses on the selling and SEO. It is therefore very important to embed images and videos with the bestselling items and they should not be placed on a single webpage. Instead the website owners should make sure that they these videos are sprinkled all over the website to get the work done so that when a search engine crawls it sees the best posts on all the pages and rank the website accordingly. Apart from SEO this practice will also answer several questions of the users and the bestselling items will be converted into HOT SELLING ITEMS.

18. Security matters a lot

If a business website is also collecting money or dealing in finance then it is very important for the owners to make sure that the trust of the website is developed among the users. It is also an SEO strategy to make sure that the best practices are carried out like display of the badges as well as other security essentials that are being used by the website to gain confidence of the users. The display of the secure SSL certificate logo will also make sure that the users never hesitates while purchasing an product via credit card as they will be sure that the information is safe and secure.

19. Including sales features

It is very important for a website owner to make sure that the sales features are included to the different pages. At times there are certain products that are out of stock and for all such products email alerts are to be created so that the users comes to know once the sale of the product is on. Other sales features include adding to wishlist, newsletter subscription, random email alerts, product updates and on spot customer services. These features are something that will make a user believe in the website and will also make sure that high conversion rates are achieved in this regard.

20. Choose the platform carefully

It is one of the most important upon which the other factors depend. Before launching a website it is very important to know that which ecommerce platform is the best so that it can be used to make sure that all the related features and plug-in are available for the website optimal view. Again, a business should never choose the platform based on cost and should make sure that the one selected is backed by serious community users and is also SEO and user friendly. The company the platform of which is being used should be active enough to answer all the questions of the users in a precise manner.

21. Creating a sitemap

To boost the rankings it is advised to create a sitemap and to submit is to all search engines that are operating over the internet. It will also allow the users to get to the desired location within the website in no time and hence the onsite time also increases. Making a good sitemap includes the overall website structure explained in detailed and easy manner so that the website can get the best to the users in any regard. The main languages that can be used in this regard are the HTML and XML as these are the top languages of the web industry and are operating at full capacity to satisfy the user needs and wants.

22. Avoid non SEO languages and technologies

There are certain languages and technologies that are considered to be non SEO and therefore it is very important to know these technologies so that the important areas of the website are kept away from them. Mainly flash and AJAX is considered to be the top two technologies in this regard. It never means that these are to be abandoned forever but it is very important to keep in view all the pages that could affect the SEO rankings negatively by using these technologies and hence those pages are to be saved to make sure that the search results are never compromised.

23. Order of products and services

Making a good order of the product and services is very important to make sure that the best results are obtained in relation to SEO. While listing the products on the SEO page it is very important to notice that the bestselling items should be ranked at the top so that they appear in the search results far before than the other items of the same genre. This order will also determine the products on the search engines and it is an advent fact that individual products are often seen appearing on Google which explains the effectiveness of the phenomenon.

24. Smart use of session ID's

It is the phenomenon that would make sure that the issue of duplicate content is never faced and on the other hand it also ensures that the website is never blacklisted in this regard. If this session ID's appear in the URL then the crawling services of the search engine make sure that the site is instantly detected and after the algorithmic update applied by Google this is not an issue at all so the SEO specialist should make sure that the issues are detected and resolved as soon as possible failing to which will become fatal results in this regard.

25. Smart use of search features

The website can attain high SEO rankings if the search features are used in the best possible way. The users should be given a chance to search the products with respect to brand name, price and popularity. Other attributes can also be added as deemed fit so that the refined results can make a product visible that is in line with the requirements of the users. All the SEO specialists should also work with the developers to make sure that these features are not only added but are maintained over a longer period of time to ensure user friendliness.

26. Power of Social media

Social media buttons should be used to make sure that it is not an issue for any user to find the business over his favorite social media network. In this regard it is recommended to add Facebook and Google+ widgets on priority as both have a very large base of daily active users and Google+ in this regard will also make sure that the groups that are created by the business also show up in search results and therefore driving more traffic towards the website and getting increased revenue for the business. In short social media should be used to increase the SEO of the website in a multidimensional manner.

27. Use of promotions to gain users

It has been seen in the past that large companies run social media campaigns to make sure that the best has been done in relation to SEO and revenue generation. In case of SEO of the website it is recommended to use the power of promotions and the services and promote then through the website to gain user attention as well as revenue in a highly positive manner. However quality should be maintained and the company should never offer substandard goods or services as a part of promotion as it could lead to customer dissatisfaction and negative rating hampering the SEO strategy.

28. Blogging power

The best service that could be used in this regard is that of Google which it has launched by the name of Blogger. This blog should be associated with the website and all the best and hot selling items should be featured time and again. Reviews of all such products and the answers to common FAQ's is something that user loves a lot and for the same reason it is also recommended to get blogging into the SEO strategy of the company. The blog can also be used for the customer services and the maintenance should be carried out 24/7.

29. Use of paid advertising

It can be done through Facebook as well as PPC advertisement. There are several advantages of using this strategy in relation to SEO and the biggest of them is that highly targeted traffic is brought to the website in this regard. It also makes sure that the customer gets the service which is highly required and desired. PPC is the phenomenon that includes banner advertisement, Ad words, Social media Ads and through buying opts in email listings. This entire paid search makes sure that the best service is provided to all the users as they are actually the laser targeted traffic that is generated.

30. Affiliate marketing

It is one of the best techniques that are used to make sure that the sales boost is acquired within a short period of time. SEO has a purpose of increasing sales and site visibility and affiliate marketing makes sure that the web presence is increased. A business should offer high commissions and should develop such products that have least return rate and this could be done only if the quality is maintained all the time in this regard. Affiliate marketing has seen a boom in recent years so it is advised to get your product featured on Clickbank and other sites that offer similar services.

31. Spam is death

It has been seen that some businesses promote the products and services through the use of spam email and trolling that is strictly prohibited by the search engines that are being used. It is also to be noted that the comments trolling if detected by Google can lead to site ban and removal from the Google's database. This also creates a sense of insecurity among the users and they are never ready to purchase the product that has been hidden within the folds of spam. It also paves a way for the cyber criminals to send similar emails to manipulate the users and their systems.

32. Email marketing

It is one of the most cost effective methods to make sure that the business is promoted and at the same time the web presence is also increased to a great extent. Buying an email list costs about $10 maximum and it is also to be noted that the best can be achieved with the help of online services like mail chimp. If the business wants to purchase an email software then it is the best deal of all times and can make sure that the emails are sent anywhere all over the world free of charge which develops cross border relation and product sales both.

33. Use the power of Google

In order to increase the web presence it is also recommended to get the best services through the use of Google Merchant center. There are millions of people all over the world that use this service of Google to find the products and services of their choice so it is advised to get all the products listed on the service so that they also appear in the organic search results of the Google and even other search engines. Signing up is very easy and if the business owns a Gmail account then it is even easier for them to get the service without any hassle.

34. Contests also do the job

If a business wants to increase the sales and create a positive buzz then it is very important for them to get the best in terms of revenue of the contests are arranged in such a manner that create a buzz on the web. Contests that are created in a well-defined and targeted manner also compel the users of others companies to take part and within no time they become the permanent customers of the new business. An increased conversion rate with highly targeted traffic is something that a contest should focus on.

35. Tracking user

In order to get the best results in terms of user behavior it is advised to all the business to track the users and the way they behave while using the website. It is also to be noted that the best and long term results can be achieved if the

SEO specialist identifies the areas of the website where user spends most of the time and then work with the developers to make those areas better and user friendly. It will increase the click through rate and will also make sure that the onsite timing of every user is increased to a great extent. It will also allow the user to remember the remarkable services that he gets from the website.

36. Client identification

It is very important to get to all those clients who are working in the best interest of the company and are loyal as well. In other words high revenue generators should be identified and they should be rewarded to make sure that in the long run they become permanent and value addition is also done in this regard. This is can be done by following simple two-step process i.e. requesting and valuing their feedback and in return offering them discounts that are granted on specific number of purchases that they would make over the website. Increased customers loyalty with quality should be the target of the business in this regard.

37. Tracking the trends

It is one of the best known sources to make sure that the web presence is increased in a way that is in line with the business requirements. Best selling products as well as the pages on which they are located should be made simple and easier for the clients so that they can buy the products with ease and satisfaction. A satisfied client is an indirect marketer of the business.

38. Multilingual appearance of the business

It is very important to notice that the more languages mean geo targeted customers as well as the overall phenomenon of the business effectiveness also increases. It is a step that should be executed while developing the business website and should be implemented to make sure that customers just feel like/at home while buying the products and services as they will know that the language they speak is being promoted through the website.

39. Choose the TLD and domain name wisely

It also boosts the web appearance as well the keyword embedded URL and country specific TLD makes sure that the SEO is laser targeted. It will also make sure that the confidence of the customers is restored. It is an advent fact that most of the customer base of the company is within the third world countries the people of which strongly believe in TLD's like .uk, .ca and .au.

40. Never say NO

NO is a word that hampers the web presence strategy of the business in a way that recovery sometimes become very difficult. It is therefore advised to all the online businesses that on order to increase the web presence and organic search of the website provide alternatives to the customers instead of saying NO. It is a highly negative impression so business should be careful.

41. Mobile friendly version

Today the era belongs to palm tops, android and IOS. It is therefore very important for the business to develop a website which has a light and mobile friendly version. The latest survey conducted by SAAS in this regard show that almost 43% of total customers buy products or services using their mobile phones so it is very important for a business to target this customer base effectively and rigorously.

42. Addition of various payment methods

It is very important for the business to make sure that the best and most secure payment methods are provided to the customers. Web based business should target the customer's confidence as it is the sole survivor guide in itself. None of the payment methods should be left and it also makes a customer believe that the business is serious regarding sales and marketing and deeply looks into the ways to increase the web presence.

43. Addition of shipping methods

Amazon serves over 150 countries all around the world and the network of the sales is expanding at a swift pace. The main reason behind this success is that they provide shipping services to all the countries they serve. For other web based ecommerce businesses it is very important to make sure that good strategies are implemented so that the customers can get goods at their doorstep boosting their reputation in a highly positive manner.

44. Effective use of robots.txt

There are various search engine spiders that analyze the website and the core of the business operations making it difficult for the business to rank the services on top. It is therefore very important for the business to use robots.txt files so that the different ecommerce activities such as add to cart, add to wishlist and successful purchase are never recorded and analyzed making it possible for the website to get the best SEO ranking.

45. Promotional pages

Whenever a promotion is launched by the business it is very important to create a separate landing page. It is never recommended to embed the page within the website. It has two very important advantages i.e. the main website will look the same way and it becomes easier for the business to get all the information and other relevant data on a separate page making it easier for the business to explain the idea.

46. Customer confusion is not a good sign

The layout of the website should be straight and simple. The user or the customers should never get confused while accessing the required information. It has been noted by various SEO organizations that in 90% cases a confused user leaves and never returns. It is therefore very important to make sure that the best view of call to action is provided so that the user's attention is focused in a positive manner.

47. Reducing shopping cart abandonment ratio

In order to reduce the shopping cart abandonment ratio it is very important for the user to make sure that the best services are provided in relation to payment options and the checkout facility. By making this facility as simple as possible the abandonment rate can be reduced which means more revenue generation and overcoming losses if any.

48. SEO and web presence audit

It should be conducted all the times making sure that the best strategy is implemented for both ideas. It is also to be noted that keywords are never same when it comes to website ranking and the related SEO techniques so it is very important to determine the keywords regularly and sprinkle them across the website in the best possible way.

49. Customer surveys

Beside tracking the customer activity on the website it is very important to note that the best services are provided to the customers after conducting surveys so that their likes and dislikes regarding the website and the related ideas is unveiled. It will also provide a sense of belonging to the customers that the business cares about them.

50. Google Ad words

It is the best keyword planner of the internet world. It makes sure that the business delves deep into the keyword search and finds highly targeted industry specific keywords in this regard. It also makes sure that the keywords that are embedded within the different pages are in line with the terms and conditions of the Google, the web giant.

51. Never go for age rank only

Some companies and businesses just go after the first page rankings on Google and in the process fail to comply with other important things. It is therefore very important to know that the sites with lower page rankings often outrank the ones on the first Google page. Business should go for services and not just SEO to boost sales.

52. Use links in a smart manner

It is very important to know that if the website uses the Java drop downs, image maps or links then the text links should be placed on the page so that the search engine spiders can follow them without any issue or problem. Being precise it is one of the most important aspects of SEO that leads to higher rankings and awesome search engine response as well.

53. Content management

The content that is being written should make sure that the main keywords are targeted in the best possible way. All the content should be unique so that search engines never detect any plagiarism and never warn the website on this. Once again each and every piece of content should be business oriented and the content writer should change the keywords to make sure that it remains up to date. In short writing for new content is never necessary as long as changing the keywords serve the purpose.

54. Meta tag management

It makes sure that the title pages of the website are clearly embedded with the keywords. According to the latest trend in the SEO industry it is very important to make sure that the Meta tag description never exceeds 150 characters and all the content written should be keyword stuffed. In case the business is using its own name as a keyword then it is practical to place it in the end so that the search results given more accurate results as people never search the business by its name especially when it is not well known.

55. Not just keywords but keywords phrases

It is important for both for web presence as well as the SEO. Keywords phrases grasp user attention and make sure that the search results are widened. Using just simple keywords also serve the purpose but if they are embedded within the keyword phrase they not only enhance the overall capability of the search result but they also make sure that more traffic is driven towards the website in an awesome way. As a general rule of thumb it is also very important to note that most of the people searching for different products and services type in keyword phrases instead of just keywords so the importance also becomes clear in this way.

56. SEO web design

The overall web layout and design is something that should be SEO oriented. It has been described earlier as well that the SEO design of the website should not be the sole focus of the website but it never means that it should be ignored totally. It is very important to know that that the search engine spiders make sure that the text files are crawled so images and flash files are never considered in this regard. It is therefore necessary to make website that is text based rather than flash and the expectations should be made clear to the developer as well so that he understands the terminologies regarding the organic search and develop and website accordingly.

57.Canonicalization is important

Before the domain name is purchased the business should decide whether to use the www or non www domains for users to land on the home page. In simple words it is very important to note that the http://www.businessname.com should lead to the main website and if http://businessname.com is used then it should also redirect to the same page under consideration. The redirecting towards the website is a very important factor and it decides the fate of the website in this regard in relation to SEO. The idea of canonicalization also decides how the external users visit the website.

58.Using home page link in a smart manner

A business should check for the homepage link throughout the website. All the external visitors should be landed on domain.com whereas if the homepage link is clicked from within the website then the people should land on domain.com/index.html to make sure that it is also linked with the domain. Instead of index.html the domain default.php can also be used in this regard and these links should always point towards the homepage so that the business website is seen time and again increasing rankings as well as the search results.

59.Never use frames

For best SEO results the developers of the websites are advised to never use the frames as there are some common issues that cannot be overcome in this regard. For instance AJAX and Flash cannot be linked to a single page with frames and therefore according to the gurus of SEO it is never advised to use AJAX and flash or if there is a need then minimum usage should be maintained in this regard.

60. File URL is never important

It is very important to note that on contrary to common belief the file URL is never a problem when it comes to the SEO. A business can use any file extension that they deem fit and the common examples in this regard are .html, .php, .htm and the list goes on. The main focus of the business should be on creating awesome SEO results and the URL file extension of any kind are crawled by the search engine spiders so they never matter.

61. Get instant spider results

If the business has developed a new website then it is important to note that the best results are the ones that are always provided by Google when it comes to search engine spiders but it is also very important to note that these results can take weeks and even over a month if the normal search form is used by the website. It is therefore necessary to note that to avoid unnecessary delays it is very important to get a link from a site that is reputable in this regard. There are thousands of websites that also provide this service at a very economical cost so the business should try to use the services of these to avoid any issues and get the website analyzed as soon as possible so that it can go live and cracking.

62. SEO is quality rather than quantity

It is very important to note that SEO is most effective if it is carried out considering quality and not quantity. For instance the back links that are sold by many website over the internet are mostly ones that are not up to the mark and therefore they never serve the purpose. It is therefore necessary to note that one quality back link can do a lot more than dozens of those that are poorly written and linked. While performing state of the art SEO quality should be focused as it is something that matters and not the quantity.

63. Keyword stuffing is fatal

While performing the site analysis search engine crawlers make sure that those terms and keywords that are within the website are determined to rank the website. Keeping this fact in view most of the websites and the SEO specialists makes sure that the keywords are stuffed within the content that is on the web pages but in most of the cases it never works and search engines deteriorate the rankings of all such websites. It is therefore advised not to stuff the website text instead perform the same practice with Meta tags written in the header of the website. Natural looking website is always ranked high and prominent.

64. Do the backlist check bi weekly

It becomes more important if the business website is hosted on the shared server. As explained before the Google and other search engines target the geo location of the website and it is very important for the business to conduct the blacklist check as if the same server is also hosting a blacklisted website then the SEO rankings of the legit site are adversely affected in this regard and if such thing happens then it is advised to change the server or if possible the company providing the hosting services.

65. Always use legit services

There are certain services that are used by many businesses around the world and these ensure that the domain name is blocked and it is never visible to the search engines. If such thing happens then it is very important to note that the Google might consider the domain as a potential spammer and block the website in the long run. Never hide any site information and domain name from any search engine as it is one of the very important aspects that are related to SEO search results.

66. Link, link and link

It means that all the websites business working with should be linked as it increases the rankings as well as compels other companies to link back and a solid SEO ground is therefore set in this regard. Linking with good and reputable companies in this regard also make sure that the best results are appeared when keywords are searched on Google and other search engines. This linking also ensures that the name of the business website also appears if the partner is searched through the related keywords hence it is a win-win situation all the way.

67. Paid links never boosts organic search

It is obvious fact that as long as the links are not included in the boy text they are of no use at all. It is therefore very important to know that the best links are the ones that are created and embedded by the dedicated SEO specialist that the business has hired. The paid links also make sure that few clicks are provided to the website and nothing else as most of the links are sponsored and are of no use.

68. Edu links are the best

It is an obvious fact that .edu domains are weighted by the search engines is also given special privileges when it comes to the search results. For a business website .edu domain are a boon and it is advised to run a search test online to see all non profit .edu domains that are looking for links or sponsors as they not only add value but also make sure that the best ranking is provided to all the sites liking to them in this regard.

69. SEO is not a one day process

It is an ongoing effort that requires daily work and it should be done to make sure that the best results are fostered. For instance an SEO specialist should make sure that the best services are provided in terms of keyword embedding and adding new keywords to the Meta tag and the text around the links and the website. Other than that the SEO also ensures that continuous efforts are applied to make sure that the organic search results remain in the favor of the website.

70. Focus on social media SEO

The power of social media in this world of advanced SEO is unquestionable. It is therefore recommended to add social media SEO in the SEO strategy of the business as it will make sure that almost half of the population of the world is reached without any effort. It can be done in easy manner and the business in this regard just needs to make sure that social media managers are hired to do the work in a good manner.

71. Making the social sharing easy

It is very important to note that social sharing is always dependent on the use of awesome posts as well as images that are embedded within the text. It is therefore advised to all the businesses to get ahead of the competitors by sharing the links of various social media platforms as it makes it easy for the customers to share the content on their walls and other pages as well. When it comes to organic search then it is very important to note that images never work but in social media SEO the scenario is totally different and therefore it is very important to add awesome and thought provoking images within the posts a business wants its customers to share.

72. Helpful content always increase the web presence

It is very important to note that the best results are obtained if the content management strategy works on creating the content that is helpful for the users. This type of content has a dual effect that is highly positive i.e. the search engines will rank the website high due to the value a piece of content provide to the user and secondly the users will also be compelled to share the content over the social media platforms making it easy and hassle free for others to get to the point or to resolve the issues of others in a far better manner.

73. Entertain the customers

Business should try to engage the audience through witty and humorous content that is always shared with them. Even of it is the use of a product or service even then it is advised to entertain the users in very possible way. It is a strong tool that increases the web presence and also makes sure that the content is shared by the customers. Nobody likes to share something that is boring and not up to the mark and therefore it is very important for the content developers to create hilarious content in this regard which makes it possible for the users to get to the root cause of the video or content in an easy manner. However the business aspect is also to be considered in this regard so that the revenue side is never ignored in this regard. Entertaining content should also be produced within the limits of professional ethics or it can also lead to web death of the business in a brutal manner.

74. Measuring the social media performance

It is important for the business to measure the social media performance just like the SEO performance to increase the web presence in an excellent manner. It is also to be noted that the every social media platform provides the related tools that are necessary to make sure that the performance is measured in an awesome manner. Using these tools can lead a business towards social media success in this regard.

75. Authorship of Google+

Google+ is by far the most important social media platform of all times and it is advised to get the best out of this platform by taking full advantage of the Google+ authorship. The business should place its logo on every post that is being shared on the website as well as on Google+. It will allow the business to get the best search results as once the keywords are searched the logo of the business will also appear on every post that has been published on the Google+ platform. Taking this feature of Meta Data authorship can lead to awesome results.

76.Owner's blogging

It is not just the duty of the social media managers or the staff to blog all the time. To increase the web presence it is also advised to all the owners and the CEO's to blog as much as they can. The idea of blogging is not hard at all and it could be done without much effort. The customers will come to know that the company is speaking itself and for the same reason they will also make sure that the problems are communicated as much as possible. On the other hand the CEO and the other top management people will come to know about the overall issues that the customers are facing in relation to the products as well as the services and they would definitely take measures that are important to save churn or customer loss in this regard.

77.Understanding SMM

SMM also known as social media marketing is a powerful tool that makes it possible for the companies t present themselves to the customers they have captured through social media. It has always been mentioned by the gurus and experts of SEO to include SMM as a part of marketing strategy as both have the same purpose i.e. to grab more customers to increase sales. It is also to be noted that the SMM is also a complete field which the business needs to focus t make sure that the best results are obtained in this regard. Business should delve deep into the subject to gain a clear insight and to make sure that they get the best results in this regard. SMM is not a one day strategy just like SEO and the related department should realize that it is a place for real and very hard work to get the desired results in favor of the business.

78. Video marketing

It is very important to note that YouTube is the best video sharing site of the world and is owned by Google but all the videos that come up in the search results of Google never belong to YouTube. For awesome video marketing and in order to increase the web presence it is advised to submit the videos to all websites like Metacafe, AOL and Yahoo just to name a few. There are regional and country based video portals as well which make sure that the best advantages are given to the video creators and submitters as they also need traffic. Business should make sure that all such websites are also captured to create cross border and regional relationships.

79. Cleaning up the code

It is very important for the SEO and web specialists to know the basic HTML and CSS codes. It will help them to clean the website code in a well-defined manner. It is a very important point due to the fact that the search engines crawlers' index the websites after taking a close look at the codes and matching them against their algorithms. If the site code is not clean the rank is automatically affected and it is due to the fact that the search engines will consider the site as spam because the code is not easily readable. SEO specialists are therefore required to clean the code as much as they can so that the rankings are made better.

80. Keeping the SEO and internet marketing knowledge up to date

SEO is not a stagnant field and therefore innovations are being developed with every passing day. SEO specialists should make sure that all these innovations are being learnt and applied in a well-defined manner. If it does not happen then it is very hard to cope with the situations these experts often face over the internet. It is also recommended to get the latest knowledge in line with the requirements of Google as it is the largest search engine of the world and satisfying it makes sure that success is not a big deal at all.

81. Outsourcing the SEO campaigns

If a business feels that the SEO strategy is not working as per expectations then it is advised to outsource the campaign as most of the outsourcing companies are working in the field very effectively. SEO companies have focus on ranking the website on the first page and if possible within the first 5 search results and they are really experts in their fields. If this is done then SEO management becomes easy and business frees itself from the hassle of in house developments. Online marketplaces such as Elance and Odesk have wide range of SEO service providers and it becomes easy for the businesses to choose the best based on rankings and past performance.

82. Sensibly naming the website images

In order to increase the web presence and SEO it is advised to use the words image and picture within the descriptions of the image that are placed on the website. It has been estimated that almost 50% of total searches that are conducted on Google include keyword plus any of the words that are mentioned so it is good for the SEO strategy overall.

83. Let Google search the website images

It is one of the most important SEO strategies and the feature can be enabled through the Google webmaster account. It allows the search engine to find the images on the website with relevant keywords. According to new search result strategy of Google this feature helps the business to enhance the SEO efforts to make the website stronger within the search results.

84. Adding user based components

In order to get the best ranking for the website it is advised to add the components the functions of which get viral over a short period of time and the effects are long lasting. Some of these components are comments from the users, sharing on social media and ratings of each and every product posted on the website. The same functionality is being used by all the social media platforms of the worlds and the success level they have achieved is in front of everyone.

85. Wide range of SEO services

Here SEO services mean the compatibility of the website with the SEO functionalities. Gone are the days when only the links were considered as the work done. In the world of today the usage of news center, emails listings, podcasts and videos is also a part of SEO strategy and it is also to be noted that the overall concept of the service has also been widened in this regard. Applying SEO with these combinations is the best strategy of all times.

86. Placing preferred URL in sitemap

At times there are some pages that the very similar to other websites and the business owners are concerned with the duplicate content issues. To avoid this issue it is advised to place the correct or preferred URL in the sitemap. It will also allow the search engines to crawl through the sitemap and index the correct URL in the search results keeping the issue far away from the SEO strategy that is in place.

87. Getting ideas from the customers

Getting the keyword ideas from the customers is one of the best practices which ensure that the site is structured according to the needs and demands of the customers. It is also to be noted that getting these ideas will also broaden the scope of the business and it will come to know that how customers search for them over the web. Product specific keywords can also be applied in this way and the best selling items can be made even better by applying the wish of the customers in terms of keywords.

88. Network building

A business should grasp the ideas of awesome web presence by connecting to the partners and by making sure that their SEO strategies are studied in full. It is also to be noted that the best SEO strategy is the one which is a combination of more than one similar plan. The business or the website should contact those partners who have already done wonders in their fields and should make sure that the related strategies are applied in a manner that is the need of the hour.

89. Providing testimonial to the partners

It is very important to note that people love honest and well written testimonials. It is therefore advised to all the businesses to ask their partners and a supplier that if they are in need of a well written testimonial and a back link of the website and if the answer is positive then the testimonial should make sure that the link to the website is included so that all everyone can see it is real

Short and concise SEO and web presence tips

90. SEO strategy can be enhanced by making sure that the back links are taken from all the websites that are using the images of the business. It is also to be noted that this service can be carried out through the Google image cache service.

91. Google alerts should be set up to make sure that instant notifications are received if there is a name of the business mentioned on any other website. The business should reach that particular website and should make sure that they are thanked.

92. Industry specific SEO specialists and bloggers should be contacted for better services and to make sure that the best services are provided to the business after hiring them if possible. Getting an industry related blogger is a boon and business should grasp this opportunity ASAP.

93. Business should make sure that the long tail keywords are embedded within the website as there is a lot of competition when it comes to short keywords and therefore other business are spending time and effort on them. Long tail keywords are easily ranked and drive same volume of traffic.

94. Keeping Google keyword planning tool is one of the best strategies that lays foundation of a strong SEO campaign. The experts in this regard are of the view that the keyword help should always be taken from this tool as it is easy to use and provides accurate results.
95. If possible the business should develop the website using the wordpress platform. There are two main reasons behind this development i.e. it is free and open source and secondly there are hundreds of plug-in that are developed to help the people in this regard saving time and energy both.
96. Blogging is also one of the SEO strategies that make sure that traffic is driven towards the website. In order to get the best results it is advised to search for all those blog topics that provide the best results and drive maximum number of users. Once these topics have been discovered then the content is to be recreated to get the maximum users on board.
97. 50% of the potential customers are lost as they are unable to find the relevant information on the website. The business should place the content exactly at that link where the customers are expecting it. The language or the development of the website does not matter as long as the content is placed to answer the customer's queries.
98. Just capturing social media is never enough. The business should make sure that each and every social media comment that is worth replying is done in a manner that is the best. As long as the customers continue to receive the sense of belonging they would love to contribute on the social media platform.

99. Business contact information should be updated as soon as there is a change. It will also make sure that the customers remain in contact and they also get a sense of belief that they are dealing with a real company. It has been observed that most of the customers first test the contact information before making an online or general purchase.

100. The business should think about the ease of the customers and not for themselves. It is therefore advised to remove all the annoying features that the customers do not like or they are bringing negative rating. Making customer experience a top priority should be the goal of the site owners and the business.

101. Last but not the least the business should be in the driving seat all the time. From content management to company policies customers should never dominate at all. It is also to be note that those software programs should be used that are understood by the owners so that if the relationship with the developers sour still the owners are able to develop and publish the content themselves.

Conclusion

SEO is not an easy task to perform and the mentioned 101 points show it all. Applying one of these of choosing a set that might interest the business is the best practice that one can follow in this regard. It is also to be noted that the best practice is the one that keeps in view the interests of business and also enhances the user experience. Before development of any website or online business it is advised to all the businesses to get the best SEO practices in place so that the issues can be overcome in this regard and in the long run the business succeeds. On the other hand it is also very important to focus on SMM and make it an integral part of the main SEO strategy of the company. It is an advent fact that organic search definitely brings traffic but in this modern era of internet marketing the social media brings users in a much fast way as compared to organic search. The companies should therefore make sure that both SEO and SMM specialists are hired in this regard and not to ask a single specialist to do both the jobs as the fields are different and same knowledge cannot be applied to both. It is also to be noted that the best strategy in this regard is the one that makes sure that the website is always ranked best and does not get obsessed by the Google page number as well as the rankings.